HISPANIC STAR

ROBERTO CLEMENTE

THE HISPANIC STAR SERIES

Read about the most groundbreaking, iconic Hispanic heroes who have shaped our culture and the world in this gripping biography series for young readers.

IF YOU CAN SEE IT, YOU CAN BE IT.

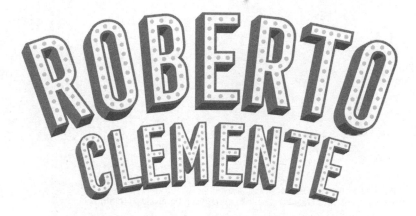

HISPANIC STAR

ROBERTO CLEMENTE

CLAUDIA ROMO EDELMAN
AND **SARA E. ECHENIQUE**

ILLUSTRATED BY **MANUEL GUTIERREZ**

ROARING BROOK PRESS

NEW YORK

Published by Roaring Brook Press
Roaring Brook Press is a division of Holtzbrinck Publishing Holdings Limited
Partnership
120 Broadway, New York, NY 10271 • mackids.com

Written by Claudia Romo Edelman and Sara E. Echenique.
Illustrated by Manuel Gutierrez.

Our books may be purchased in bulk for promotional, educational, or business
use. Please contact your local bookseller or the Macmillan Corporate
and Premium Sales Department at (800) 221-7945 ext. 5442 or by email at
MacmillanSpecialMarkets@macmillan.com.

Library of Congress Cataloging-in-Publication Data is available.

First edition, 2022
Book design by Samira Iravani
Printed in the United States of America by Lakeside Book Company, Crawfordsville,
Indiana

ISBN 978-1-250-82810-1 (paperback)
10 9 8 7 6 5 4 3 2 1

ISBN 978-1-250-82808-8 (hardcover)
10 9 8 7 6 5 4 3 2 1

For my mom, who lost her battle to Covid, but whose values live in me every day. I am who I am because she was the best of role models.

For my husband, Richard, and children, Joshua and Tamara, who surround me with their love, their belief in me, and support. They make it all possible.

Most of all, this series is dedicated to the children of tomorrow. We know that you have to see it to be it. We hope these Latino heroes teach you to spread your wings and fly.
—C. R. E.

Para mamá y papá, por todo.
—S. E.

CHAPTER ONE

A LEGEND IS BORN

"Roberto was born to play baseball."

—LUISA WALKER, Roberto's mother

On a rainy summer day in 1934, on a small Caribbean archipelago—a group of islands—with the Atlantic Ocean above it, the Caribbean Sea below, and mountains towering in the middle, a future baseball legend was born.

Roberto Enrique Clemente Walker entered the world with no shortage of love in his life. He was the youngest of seven children in a close-knit community in Carolina, Puerto Rico. Thirty-eight short years later, he would be mourned and revered by countless Puerto Ricans and other Latinx and baseball fans around the world as one of the greatest baseball players and humanitarians (someone who does good) to ever live.

Like many Latinx children, Roberto's name tells the

story of his family. In Puerto Rican and other Latinx cultures, children use both of their parents' last names, not just one. *Clemente* came from his father, Melchor Clemente, and *Walker* came from his mother, Luisa Walker. When he moved to the mainland United States as an adult, some people thought Roberto's "real" last name was Walker, because it went last. But for most of his career on the mainland United States, he would go by Roberto Clemente.

Melchor Clemente was fifty-one when his youngest child was born. Melchor was born in 1882, less than ten years after Spain technically ended enslavement in Puerto Rico. Enslavement in the mainland United States had ended only a few years before that.

Melchor was a no-nonsense man who supported his family by working hard as a foreman at a sugarcane processing company. He was a short man, often seen with his straw hat and the machete he used to work with sugarcane. Like Roberto, Melchor had rich dark brown skin and serious brown eyes.

Luisa Walker was from Loíza, Puerto Rico. She was the first of many strong women who would shape Roberto's life. By the time she had Roberto, Luisa's life had already been marked by tragedy, and it would not be the last time.

Before Luisa married Melchor, her first husband, the

father of her two oldest children, Luis and Rosa, had passed away. Despite their hardships, Luisa created a warm and welcoming household for their family. She worked harder than anyone, including Melchor. Cooking, cleaning, washing clothes, educating and raising the children fell to her, as it did to many women at the time. Luisa also sewed and cooked for the sugarcane workers to earn money. She made one of the front rooms of their modest house a makeshift grocery store. On the weekends, she sold meat. Luisa had powerful shoulders and arms that could lift the carcass of a full cow and butcher it—strength that Roberto would inherit. When talking about his mother, Roberto would later say she never had time for dancing. But she taught her children to find joy in life and in the little things.

When Luisa and Melchor were raising their family, much like today, Puerto Ricans were Black, brown, white, and every possible combination in between, many times all within the same family. That's because Puerto Ricans come from three main groups of ancestors: Taínos, Spaniards, and Africans.

Taínos, farmers and hunter-gatherers who originally lived in Puerto Rico, became the dominant culture in approximately 1000 CE, more than one thousand years ago. They referred to the Puerto Rican archipelago as Borinquen (sometimes also called Boriken or Boriquen). *Borinquen* and many of the words and names Taínos used more than a thousand years ago are still used today. If you've ever read or spoken about a juracán (hurricane), canoa (canoe), iguana, hamaca (hammock), or manatí (manatee), then you've been using Taíno words.

Taínos also had their own ball game, known as batu, which they played on the batey, a ball field they used for special ceremonies. The game involved throwing a ball made out of resin (almost like a plant-made glue) and leaves to a player who would hit the ball with a bat that looked like an oar. Some people who study language believe that the words for "bat" in Spanish (*bate* and *batear*) come from the Taíno words *batey* and *batu*.

Taínos lived in small villages known as yucayeques led by their caciques, or chiefs. From 1000 CE until 1492, when Christopher Columbus and his Spanish crew invaded Puerto Rico, there was a female chief, known as a cacica. According to local legend, the Spanish baptized Yuiza, the cacica, and she changed her name to Loíza. This later became the name of the town where Roberto Clemente's mother was born many years later.

When Columbus landed in Borinquen, he began referring

to it as San Juan Bautista in honor of an important Catholic saint believed by Catholics to have baptized Jesus Christ. But once the Spaniards realized there was gold on the island, they began referring to it as Puerto Rico, or "rich port," and renamed the capital city San Juan.

The Spaniards were not kind to the Taínos and thought less of them because they did not act like them or have the same weapons. The Taínos, who had never met people who acted or looked like the Spaniards, were no match for Spanish guns or germs. The Spaniards mined gold and grew sugarcane, tobacco, and coffee in Puerto Rico, all of which require a lot of hard work in the Puerto Rican heat. Instead of paying for this labor, the Spanish decided to force people to work against their will, enslaving the Taínos. Shortly after, the Spanish brought boats full of other enslaved individuals taken from their homes on the African continent against their will to Puerto Rico and other places, where they were also treated horribly.

Loíza became a home for escaped enslaved people, known as cimarrones, especially those from the Nigerian Yoruba tribe who the Spanish had kidnapped. The cimarrones ran away from Spanish enslavers, hid from the Spanish army in dense mangroves, and formed their own community. Today, Loíza still has one of the largest populations of Black Puerto Ricans and celebrates a rich history of dance and music (such as bomba and plena), food, and fiestas patronales—special celebrations commemorating saints from the Catholic faith brought by the Spanish, since they did not allow enslaved people to celebrate their own faiths. Loízan and Puerto Rican culture include countless traditions inherited from these African ancestors.

In 1898, when Melchor Clemente was fifteen years old, the Spanish left Puerto Rico, and the United States of America took over control.

A BRIEF HISTORY OF SLAVERY IN PUERTO RICO

On March 22, 1873, leaders of the Puerto Rican abolitionist movement won a long battle against slavery on the archipelago. The Spanish National Assembly had finally abolished slavery, ending nearly four hundred years of the practice in Puerto Rico.

Slavery came with the Spanish colonizers in the sixteenth century shortly after they arrived on the shores of Puerto Rico in 1493. The Spaniards first enslaved the indigenous Taino people to work in their mines searching for gold, but it wasn't until the first half of the nineteenth century that the archipelago saw a substantial increase in its enslaved population, including people forcibly brought from their homes in Africa. In 1815, Spain sought to create a profitable export economy in its colony by opening Puerto Rican ports to foreign trade and encouraging immigration. Foreign planters arrived and imported forced labor from neighboring islands and Africa to work their fields, especially sugarcane. Demand for sugar in the United States was growing, and planters used forced labor to increase their profits. By 1841 Puerto

Rico had forty-one thousand enslaved people, up from seventeen thousand in 1812.

Over the years, enslaved people led many revolts and joined the first major revolt against Spanish colonial rule, called the Grito de Lares ("Cry of Lares") for the town where the uprising took place. Although slavery was abolished in 1873, Puerto Ricans continued to revolt against colonial rule, even after Spain conceded the territory of Puerto Rico to the United States during the Spanish-American War peace treaty negotiations in 1898.

Roberto Enrique Clemente Walker was born to Melchor Clemente and Luisa Walker in Carolina, Puerto Rico, on August 18, 1934, during the Great Depression (1929–1939). At the time, there was great poverty and challenges across the United States and its territories, but Melchor and Luisa always made sure their seven children had basic necessities. They collected drinking water in a container on their kitchen roof, and the children always had food. Their family did not have a lot, but they had each other and felt they had enough. Roberto was the youngest of the seven children in the close-knit family. His parents worked hard, put their family first, and always served their communities. As an adult, Roberto later said, "We used to get together at night, and we would sit down and make jokes and eat whatever we have to eat. And this was something wonderful to me."

Roberto was very close to his brothers and sisters, but their bond could not protect him from the many losses he would suffer during his life.

Roberto encountered tragedy very early on. When he was still a baby, his older sister Anairis was playing outside their house near a large open fire that their mother used to cook for sugarcane workers. Anairis's dress caught on fire, and a few days later she passed away at a nearby hospital. Roberto may not have remembered his sister, but she was a constant presence in his life. He would say, "I can feel Anairis at my side."

As he grew, Roberto proved to be a bright, curious child. He wanted to know how things worked and why. He took time and care to do things his way. When his family interrupted him, he would often respond with "momentito, momentito." *Just a moment, wait a moment.* One of his older cousins started calling him "Momen," and the nickname stuck. Even though Roberto took his time, he was anything but slow. He played outside all day long, running and getting faster and stronger every day. He was so strong and fast that when he was twelve, he ran across a highway in Carolina and pulled a fully grown man to safety from a burning car.

In his short life, Roberto grew from a strong, passionate kid into an adult who taught others about the power of perseverance and the importance of respect, and that true leadership comes from caring for others. He inspired people to dream of possibilities beyond what they had ever known and to achieve those dreams honorably.

CHAPTER TWO

AN UNDENIABLE TALENT

"Clemente could field the ball in New York
and throw a guy out in Pennsylvania."

—VIN SCULLY, baseball announcer

As a kid, Roberto was like many of us. He went to school; he spent time with his family and friends. In his downtime, he liked to read magazines and watch movies, and he loved to play games. No one could have known that the Puerto Rican kid asking for a momentito would one day be one of the greatest baseball players to ever live. Or that the shy kid who tried not to call attention to himself would one day have entire schools, stadiums, and awards named after him.

Before he played baseball in the major leagues, with access to the world's best bats and balls and players, Roberto played with any bat and ball he could get his hands on. He loved the sport so much, he would practice with any equipment he could find, and could turn anything into a game of baseball. He used guava branches and broomsticks as bats. He made homemade balls out of paper or rubber (much like the Taínos) and used tennis balls or any other balls he could find. He sometimes even used bottle caps instead of balls, which helped him develop his incredible aim and coordination. When he wasn't playing, he'd be thinking about playing. One time, as a punishment, his mother tried to burn his bat, but luckily the bat survived and Roberto kept playing. His big hands and strong body were helpful in becoming good at baseball, but his dedication is ultimately what made him so great.

By the time Roberto was born, Puerto Rico no longer formally had enslavement, and the people who ran the government thought all of Puerto Rico and its Black, brown, and white people were treated the same. In reality, lighter-skinned Puerto Ricans (then and now) had more wealth and more opportunities than darker-skinned Puerto Ricans, much like white and Black people in the mainland United States. But in Puerto Rico, many Puerto Ricans like to pretend this is not a problem. When Roberto's mother, Luisa, was pregnant with Roberto, his older sister Anairis was excited to have a new baby sibling. But she hoped he would be born white. When he was born, Anairis said, "Here he is—a little dark."

DESCENDED FROM LIBERTOS

The first Black people arrived in Puerto Rico as libertos, "free men," with the Spaniards, and throughout the centuries of slavery, libertos outnumbered the enslaved population in the archipelago. Their numbers grew as the Spanish monarchy had issued a Royal Decree of Graces, which established new rules for the slave trade in Spanish colonies, adding restrictions to the granting of freedom to enslaved people. That same year, a new slave code was introduced, under which enslaved people could buy their freedom, or that of their children, if an owner was willing to sell it to them. By the mid-1800s free Black people made up more than 40 percent of Puerto Rico's population. Many who were able to buy their freedom, called "freedmen," started settlements in the towns of Santurce, Carolina, Canóvanas, Loíza, and Luquillo, where they worked as tradespeople. Some became slave owners themselves. Long after slavery was abolished, these towns would remain segregated.

Today, many in Puerto Rico say they are racially mixed, and some don't feel the need to identify as being from any specific race. Even so, colorism and racism are often hidden within the archipelago's culture, classifying people by the shade of their skin and giving privilege to affluent communities that present as being predominantly white.

When Roberto was growing up, one of his older brothers, Justino (whose nickname was "Matino"), played in a top amateur baseball league in Puerto Rico. At the time, professional baseball in the United States was still segregated. This meant that white people did not allow Black players like Matino to play in the league just because of the color of their skin, no matter how talented they were. Matino was Roberto's first baseball teacher and helped spark his passion for the game. Later, when Roberto had proven himself to be one of the greatest baseball players to ever live, he would insist that his brother Matino was the best baseball player in the family.

During Roberto's childhood, Black baseball players in the mainland United States established the Negro League to counter the professional league's racist practices. Many of the league's best players traveled to Puerto Rico to play for teams like the San Juan Senadores (Senators) and the Santurce Cangrejeros (Crabbers) in the Puerto Rican winter league. The Puerto Rican professional baseball league, also known as the winter league, was founded in 1938 with six island teams. Over time, the league became known for hosting up-and-coming players. It is credited for launching the careers of several major league talents, including many Negro League players. The league also allowed current Major League players to train and stay fresh. Some of baseball's greatest players spent their off-season in Puerto Rico playing ball.

During the winter league, Puerto Rican children like Roberto had the chance to watch some of the greatest baseball players in the world. And much like other children in Puerto Rico, he idolized players in the Puerto Rican winter league and went to any game he could. He would ride the bus from Carolina, when his parents could afford the extra twenty-five cents for the bus fare and game ticket. One player in particular stood out for Roberto as a superstar: Monte Irvin.

Monford Merrill "Monte" Irving was a Black player from the Negro League who had been unfairly denied a place in the major league. Born in Alabama, Monte had grown up in New Jersey and played several varsity sports, including football and track and field. After he was recruited by Negro League baseball teams in college, he played left field for the Newark Eagles in the regular season and the San Juan Senadores in the winter season.

Roberto would do anything to see his idol, Monte Irvin, play. He later said, "I never had enough nerve, I didn't want to even look at him straight in the face . . . But when he passed by I would turn around and look at him because I idolized him." When he could not afford to buy a ticket, he and his friends would find ways to get in for free. Monte and other players would let Roberto and his friends carry their bags to get onto the field. Eventually, Roberto and Monte became friends, despite Roberto's shyness. Monte

NEGRO LEAGUE BASEBALL

Black Americans have been playing baseball since the late 1800s, but racism and segregation had forced them off white professional teams by 1900. So Black players formed their own teams, traveling from place to place, playing with anyone who was willing.

In 1920 in Kansas City, Missouri, a few owners of these independent teams in the Midwest joined hands to organize the Negro National League under the guidance of former Black pitcher Andrew "Rube" Foster, the owner of the Chicago American Giants. Soon, other team owners organized Negro leagues in the South and East. Organized Black baseball eventually spread to Canada and Latin America.

In the Negro leagues, baseball players of color were able to maintain a high level of professional skill, showing that they could play on even terms with white teams, and even contributed to the economic development of Black communities. Black baseball remained popular until 1947, when Jackie Robinson made his debut with the Brooklyn Dodgers.

would make sure Roberto got into the games and once gifted Roberto his own ball and glove.

Monte later said he liked playing in Puerto Rico more than the mainland United States for many reasons, including that he was treated much better than on the mainland, where segregation was still the law of the land. In Puerto Rico, he and other players were treated like celebrities, offered home-cooked meals and other gifts by their fans.

When Roberto was about thirteen years old, the Montreal Royals called up Jackie Robinson—a Black baseball player—to play in the major leagues. This was the beginning of the end of segregation in baseball, though racism among the audience and other players was still rampant. Two years later, Monte Irvin was also called to the major leagues to play for the New York Giants. These were important moments for Roberto, who lived and breathed baseball, but whose own older brother had been denied a chance to play on the mainland because of the color of his skin. Jackie's and Monte's successes allowed Roberto and other young Black Puerto Rican boys the chance to dream that they could also play baseball in the big leagues.

Roberto was shy in high school, often sitting quietly in the back of the classroom. He was smart and curious, as he had always been, but he was not loud about who he was. At fourteen, Roberto was chosen to play in a men's amateur softball league named Sello Rojo (Red Seal) after their sponsor, the Sello Rojo rice packaging company. At sixteen, he started playing with the local professional team from Juncos.

In 1952, when he was just eighteen years old, the Cangrejeros de Santurce, one of Puerto Rico's winter league teams, signed Roberto to play professional baseball, offering to pay him $40 a week. Roberto was still in high school at the time and had to switch schools because his former school would not let him play.

The Cangrejeros won the Puerto Rican championship that year, and word started to spread about Roberto Clemente, the team's new talented young player.

Melchor would watch his son proudly from the stands, but he did not know the basics of baseball or understand the purpose of the game. Often people who have to work so hard to survive do not have time for anything else, as was the case for Melchor. He felt sorry for his son for having to run around the bases after hitting the ball, while other hitters got to sit back down at the bench after striking out.

During this time, even though Roberto was playing baseball every day, he somehow made time to explore sports beyond baseball. Much like Monte Irvin, Roberto

threw the javelin and ran in track-and-field events at his
high school. His powerful left arm and explosive speed
began to develop during this time, so much so that people
thought he could compete with the Puerto Rican Olympic
team. Playing track and field helped Roberto develop his
baseball game—it made him stronger, faster, and nimbler. Roberto said that his strong throwing arm devel-
oped in part from throwing the javelin in high school but

that he truly inherited his strength from his mother. As an adult, he later said, "My mother has the same kind of an arm, even today at seventy-four." While it's true that Roberto's build made it possible for him to practice a variety of sports, it was his drive to work harder and practice more than anyone else that made him one of the most powerful baseball players to ever live.

PUERTO RICO'S NATIONAL OLYMPIC COMMITTEE

Although Puerto Rico is part of the United States as its territory, the International Olympic Committee (IOC) recognizes Puerto Rico as being separate from the US, and in January 1948, the IOC allowed the archipelago's team to compete in the Olympic Games for the first time. Since then, Puerto Rican athletes have been able to compete in Summer and Winter Olympics.

In Puerto Rico, Roberto played with professional baseball players from the mainland, including both Black and white players. Even though Puerto Rico was more welcoming to

Black players like Monte Irvin, its problems with colorism continued. Roberto was not immune to them, even in his personal life. As a young teenager, Roberto had a girlfriend who broke up with him simply because her family thought he was too dark.

When Roberto began playing professional baseball with the Cangrejeros, word got around about a kid playing baseball who scouts "had to look out for." One player said, "If you could cut it in Puerto Rico, you could be in the big leagues within a year." Just a little over a year after Roberto signed with the Cangrejeros, this proved to be true for him as well.

Puerto Rico's baseball league was a source of new talent for baseball scouts from many Major League teams. In November 1952 the Brooklyn Dodgers held tryouts in Puerto Rico. The Brooklyn Dodgers were the same team that had desegregated big-league baseball by signing Jackie Robinson just five years before.

JACKIE ROBINSON BREAKS THE "COLOR LINE"

It's April 15, 1947, a beautiful day for baseball, and the Brooklyn Dodgers are set to play the Boston Braves at Ebbets Field in Brooklyn, New York. The Dodgers run out of the dugout and take the field. It's a moment that, on the surface, looks like every other opening day in baseball history. But it changed the game and the world.

At first base stood twenty-eight-year-old Jackie Robinson. Up until this game in 1947, Black players had not been allowed to play in the Major League. Jackie Robinson changed all that and broke the baseball "color line," ushering in a new era, not just in the sport but in a burgeoning civil rights movement that would come to a head twenty years later.

Three months after Jackie Robinson broke the color barrier, more Black players began playing Major League Baseball, namely Larry Doby of the Cleveland Indians and Hank Thompson and Willard Brown of the St. Louis Browns. (Called Ese Hombre in Puerto Rico, Willard Brown won the Triple Crown in the Puerto Rican winter league twice, leading the league in batting average, home runs, and runs batted in.) These men paved the way for talented athletes from all different backgrounds for many generations.

Roberto was one of roughly seventy players at the tryout, and he was one of the best. He could throw, he could run, he could catch, and he could most certainly hit. And he did it all better than most of the players out there. Roberto was the rare player who presented a major threat. One scout found he had "all the tools and likes to play" and called him "a real good-looking prospect!"

Fifteen months later, Roberto had graduated from high school, and that scout got his wish. In 1954, at least five teams saw Roberto play and knew they wanted him for their teams. Roberto badly wanted to play professional baseball for the Brooklyn Dodgers, the same team that had jump-started Jackie Robinson's career a few years before.

On February 19, 1954, Melchor sent a telegram to Brooklyn, New York: I WILL SIGN A CONTRACT ON BEHALF OF MY SON ROBERTO CLEMENTE FOR THE SEASON 1954. FOR THE SALARY OF FIVE THOUSAND ($5,000.00) FOR THE SEASON PLUS A BONUS OF $10,000 signed by MELCHOR CLEMENTE, FATHER and ROBERTO CLEMENTE, SON[.]

The Dodgers signed Roberto to their minor league team, the Montreal Royals, which funneled its most talented players to the Dodgers. They wanted Roberto to play for the Royals until he was ready for the Dodgers, and expected he would be able to do so within a few years, just like Jackie Robinson had done before him.

Although other teams offered Roberto more money, he had given the Dodgers his word that he would play for them, and he turned down the other teams. The conditions of his contract made Roberto eligible for the draft, which meant any team that wanted him could have him. But once the season started, Roberto barely played while with the Royals, so who would want a player that did not play?

Roberto began planning his travel from Puerto Rico to Florida for training. And he had no idea what was coming.

CHAPTER THREE

MOVING UP NORTH

**"This one throws a bullet from center on the fly.
I couldn't believe my eyes."**

—AL CAMPANIS, Brooklyn Dodgers' scout

When he left for spring training in 1954, nineteen-year-old Roberto left his family and Puerto Rico for the first time in his life. He had never been on a plane before, and he was very nervous. It turned out he did not like flying.

Roberto's first stop off the island was in Florida, where the Montreal Royals had their spring training.

When he arrived at spring training, Roberto was the team's youngest player, one of only two Black players and one of only two Spanish-speaking players. Although he had learned English in high school, he did not use it often in Puerto Rico and felt more comfortable speaking Spanish. Some people took his quietness to mean he did not understand them, but Roberto was very perceptive and understood more English than he spoke. He also knew who he was, just like when he was a child asking for a "momentito, momentito." One well-known maker of bats heard about Roberto and reached out to him to help him choose his equipment. Roberto had his signature *Momen Clemente* engraved on his first bats in the league.

Roberto was prepared to play, but he was not prepared for life on the mainland. During spring training he confronted the South's segregation for the first time. In Florida, and elsewhere in the southern United States, laws separated Black and white people in almost every possible way—schools, libraries, bathrooms, restaurants, buses, trains, and more were all built to exclude Black people. Roberto was already shy by nature and feeling alone as one of the few Black and Spanish-speaking players. But this formal segregation was something completely unfamiliar to him.

In Puerto Rico, he knew some people judged him because of his skin color, but he had never been denied a seat at a restaurant because of how he looked. And to make it worse, his white teammates did not seem to notice or care. This was normal for them, and they expected him to be okay with it.

But it wasn't normal for Roberto or other Puerto Rican and Latinx players, who came from less overtly segregated homes.

Victor "Vic" Pellot Power was another Black Puerto Rican baseball player who'd joined the league around the same time as Roberto, in 1954. Throughout his career, Vic Power played for teams in the American League, including the Cleveland Indians, Minnesota Twins, and Los Angeles Angels. He would later say that in Puerto Rico, "We were all together . . . We went to school together. We danced together. A lot of Black Puerto Ricans marry white women. When I get there—the States—I don't know what to do." Vic would use humor to deflect how uncomfortable and painful segregation on the mainland was. When a waitress told him that the restaurant he was in did not serve Black people, Vic replied, "That's okay, I don't eat [Black people]. I just want some rice and beans."

Roberto had a different type of personality. He was passionate but serious. He not only gave respect, he expected it in return. Unfortunately, his first time on the mainland United States felt anything but respectful. When Roberto would travel for games with the team, they would often go to segregated areas in the United States, where the team forced him and the other Black players who joined the team over time to stay in different places than the white players. Restaurants refused to let him sit at their tables or eat their food. Roberto and his nonwhite teammates were made to wait on the bus while his white teammates ate and later brought him and the other Black players milk and sandwiches from those restaurants.

Roberto was furious. Not just with such unfair laws, or with the restaurants for their unjust treatment, but also

with his teammates, who ate at these restaurants and gave them their money even though they knew how badly these places treated Roberto and the other Black players. Roberto was a proud person, and he stood up for people who were not treated fairly, but no one stood up for him or his other teammates. It was not fair, and it was not right.

Roberto was not able to express how he felt to his mostly English-speaking white teammates, but they could tell he was not happy. So Roberto stood up for himself when he could he could not change the laws or the minds of restaurant owners and workers on his own, but he refused to be treated like that.

Roberto traveled to Montreal, Canada, after spring training. Puerto Rico and Montreal were different in many ways. Puerto Rico is a warm, small island archipelago in the Caribbean, with year-round heat and humidity and full of Spanish speakers. Montreal is the largest city in the province of Quebec, Canada, most of the people in the community spoke French, and it was *cold*. For the first time, Roberto felt freezing temperatures and touched snow.

But Montreal and Puerto Rico were also quite similar in other ways. Much like Puerto Rico, Montreal did not have formal segregation between people of different skin colors. But also like Puerto Rico, people treated Black and brown people worse than white people just because of how they looked. Roberto did not have many friends in Montreal, but on one occasion he went out with a white woman, and an older lady yelled at them just for being together.

Roberto tried to focus on baseball, the only reason he was there, but instead of playing Roberto and helping to develop his skills for a move up to the Dodgers, the Royals kept him hidden, not allowing him to play during games. They did not want other teams to know how talented he was because they were afraid that those other teams would convince him to play for them. If Roberto played well and hit the ball, the coach would bench him and make him sit out games. Scouts came to Montreal's games but rarely got to see Roberto on the field. Roberto was ready to pack up and go back home, where at least he knew he would play.

Even though Roberto did not play as much as he would have liked or expected to, his talent was indisputable. Montreal's trick hid Roberto's talent from a lot of people, but anyone who saw Roberto play—even at his worst— knew he had a special gift.

A scout for the Pittsburgh Pirates, a Major League Baseball team, saw Roberto during practice. The scout had arrived during the team's pregame workout, a visit intended to observe a Royals pitcher, and when he saw Roberto throwing, he "couldn't take [his] eyes off him." He was impressed with Roberto's powerful throws and hits. When Roberto played as a pinch-hitter, the scout "liked his swing." Asking around, the scout found out Roberto was eligible for the draft. After one particularly frustrating day for Roberto, the scout found him and told him to stay right where he was. The Pirates wanted Roberto even if the Royals and Dodgers did not appreciate him.

That year, the Pittsburgh Pirates were the worst team in their league. Since he knew the Pirates were slated to be in last place, the scout decided then and there that Roberto would be their first draft pick. Too excited to keep his intentions a secret, the scout told Max Macon, the Royals manager, "to take good care of 'our boy' and see that he didn't get hurt." Macon reportedly responded, "Clemente? He's nothing!" in a poor attempt at dissuading the Pirates from drafting Roberto.

The Pirates scout was true to his word, and on November 22, 1954, the Pirates chose their first draft pick. The player the Pittsburgh Pirates most wanted out of anyone was the unknown player sitting on the bench in Montreal: Roberto Clemente. A team representative told the shocked roomful of sportswriters, "He can run and throw—and we think he can hit."

WHAT IS A DRAFT?

A draft is when sports teams in a league are allowed to pick which players they'd like to have play for them during the season. This works similarly for baseball, basketball hockey, and American football. During the draft, teams take turns to select players who are eligible to play in a league, and the team can then give those players contracts to play for them.

Signing on with the Pittsburgh Pirates was the silver lining Roberto needed after his wildly disappointing season in Montreal. Roberto returned to Puerto Rico to play in the winter league and rejoin his family, friends, and community.

On December 30, 1954, following a series of winter league games on the southern coast of Puerto Rico, Roberto skipped the team's bus home and drove back with two of his brothers. The day before, doctors had operated on Roberto's eldest brother, Luis, because of a brain tumor. Roberto and his brothers drove north to see him, but it was late at night and very dark. An irresponsible driver who had been drinking alcohol chose to drive that night and ran right through a red light. He drove right into Roberto's car.

Although his brothers were not hurt, Roberto injured his neck and spine. He had his mind set on seeing his hospitalized brother, so he kept driving. These injuries caused him a lot of pain at the time and never fully went away. Roberto made it in time to see his brother, but unfortunately Luis passed away the next day, on New Year's Eve. This would not be the last child Luisa, Roberto's mother, and his family would lose so tragically.

Roberto kept playing through his sadness and won the 1955 Serie Mundial del Caribe— the Caribbean World Series—with the Cangrejeros de Santurce.

Once the season was over, Roberto had to pack up again for spring training in Florida—this time with the Pittsburgh Pirates.

He encountered segregation again, though this time he knew what to expect.

Again, restaurants, hotels, golf courses, and people rejected him and others because they were Black. Again, his teammates did not defend or protect him, even though many of them lived in the North, where formal segregation was not normal. He was the top draft pick, but he could not even stay in the same hotel as his white teammates. Instead, Roberto and other Black players stayed with local families who took them in. Roberto and others were fed up with how Black and other nonwhite people were being treated.

Eventually, the team got Roberto and the other Black players a station wagon, so when they traveled they did not have to wait on the bus while the white players ate inside. Small, but not meaningless, change.

CHAPTER FOUR

BASEBALL AND THE CIVIL RIGHTS MOVEMENT

"He had a problem with people who treated you differently because of where you were from, your nationality, your color, also poor people, how they were treated . . . that's the thing I really respected about him most, was his character, the things he believed in."

—AL OLIVER, Pittsburgh Pirate 1968–77

Even though he was sad to leave his family, in pain from the car accident, and still mourning the loss of his brother, Roberto committed to being the best baseball player he could be. He channeled how he felt into baseball. He pushed himself to become even stronger, faster, and nimbler.

Out in right field, Roberto had a magnificent ability to catch balls others could not. His hands were so "magical" they were said to have "eyes at their fingertips." Players dreaded hitting baseballs in Roberto's direction—no matter how fast a ball was going, Roberto could track it, sprint to it at full speed, catch it, then turn around to throw it back to teammates, all before the hitter could run from one base to the next. During one game against the Giants, Roberto darted after the ball, slammed into the concrete field wall out in left field, and fell to the ground. The stadium was silent as Roberto stood up, blood gushing from his chin (it took six stitches to close!), and held up his glove to show the ball safely inside it. The fans went wild. Local Pittsburgh Pirate fans began to recognize Roberto as a star on the team, and he gave his all for them every single game.

Roberto also hit with the precision he learned as a kid playing baseball with sticks and bottle caps. He had a wildly strong swing, different from other players in the professional leagues but incredibly effective. He loved to hit what others called "bad balls" and would say, "They're not bad if I hit them." When Roberto hit a ball, he would burst with speed from base to base. In 1956 he hit the first recorded inside-the-park grand slam—a home run with players on all three bases—and the fans loved it.

Roberto played hard every single game he played, even if the game was not considered important by his other teammates. He knew what it meant to his fans, in Puerto Rico and in Pittsburgh, for him to play. Altogether, this meant that Roberto pushed his body to the limit every day he played, and that often meant he was in pain.

He never fully recovered from the car accident, and he had a lot of pain in his back throughout his entire career. Roberto studied his own body the same way he studied baseball. He could tell exactly what was wrong or not quite right. He could feel when it was too danger- ous for him to play through an injury. But his coach and others did not always agree he should sit out games because of the pain. Sports journalists—people who write news about sports—in particular were mean about his injuries and made fun of how he felt and how he spoke.

When Roberto was just a rookie player for the Pitts- burgh Pirates, before he earned his well-deserved records and awards, many important people in baseball did not think much of him. Most people in baseball at the time were also white, and even if they did not admit it, they were more critical of Roberto because he was Black, Latino, and did not speak English the same way they did (never mind that he spoke two languages, while they spoke only one). Although reporters took white players' injuries seriously, they made Roberto's pain a running joke. One reporter delighted in listing all the many painful injuries and maladies Roberto suffered:

> In his time, Clemente has been bothered not only by the usual pulled muscles, but also by tension headaches, nervous stomach, a tendon rubbing against the bone in his left heel, malaria, a strained instep, bone chips in his elbow, a curved spine, countless bruises, one leg heavier than the other (according to a chiropractor), hematoma (a type of bruise) of the thigh incurred in a lawn-mowing accident, wayward discs in his neck and back, a systemic paratyphoid infection from the hogs on a small farm he owns, severe food poisoning, and insomnia . . . Writers report that Clemente has to 'boop' his back and neck into place every morning before getting out of bed.

Because reporters focused on his injuries, they did not report on his abilities and downplayed how talented he was. They also wrote about him in ways that confirmed their own misinformed opinions about what a "Latin player" would be, regardless of who Roberto was as a person. They made fun of his accent in English, often quoting him in ways that made him sound unintelligent. Monolingual players, those who spoke only English, also had accents and used incorrect grammar, but reporters corrected their mistakes when quoting them and made them sound more intelligent.

To make matters worse, these writers would not report on Roberto's incredible athletic feats, even though they wrote about players who were much less skilled. Roberto later said, "Lots of times I have the feeling people want to take advantage of me, especially writers . . . They talk to me, but maybe they don't like me, so they write about me the way they want to write."

Roberto also said, "It didn't matter that the Latino ball player was good, but for the mere fact of his not being North American he was marginalized . . . They have an open preference for North Americans. Mediocre players received immense publicity while true stars are not highlighted as they deserve."

Many sports journalists and even the main baseball card company often referred to Roberto by the English nickname Bob or Bobby, but Roberto rejected those attempts to change who he was. He insisted he be called Roberto. The myth goes that Roberto even chose his Pirate number—the number 21—for the number of letters in his full name: R-O-B-E-R-T-O C-L-E-M-E-N-T-E W-A-L-K-E-R.

In 1960 the Pittsburgh Pirates—once the worst team in the league—played in the World Series against the New York Yankees. Roberto's mother flew for the first time to see him play. His father was too afraid of flying to come, but watched proudly from Puerto Rico.

Few people thought the Pirates could win, and most fans outside of Pittsburgh and Puerto Rico did not know who Roberto was. Pittsburgh fans knew Roberto, and during the series, Roberto kept with him a trophy given to him by Pirates fans who had named him their most popular player. Of all the incredible players in that series, Roberto was the only one to hit in all seven games. Roberto was the first player from the Caribbean and Latin America to start in a World Series. After many ups and downs, good games and bad, the Pirates won the World Series in the seventh game.

And in true Roberto fashion, he planned to use the bonus he earned in the World Series to buy Luisa a house in Puerto Rico.

When he returned to Puerto Rico, he was greeted by hundreds of people at the airport welcoming him home. Parties and balls were held in his honor, and he received an award for the most outstanding Latin American player in the major leagues. But on the mainland United States his talent still went largely unrecognized.

In November of that year, the Baseball Writers' Association of America announced the winner of the National League's most valuable player. Roberto was not named the first-, second-, or even third-most valuable player—he was named the eighth, despite having played an incredible season and even more incredible World Series. This decision frustrated and infuriated Roberto, but worst of all, it hurt his pride.

Roberto had spent his life working hard and believing in himself—how else would he have ended up in the professional leagues as the youngest player on the team? And he was not used to giving up just because something was difficult. Over time, Roberto found small ways to force systemic change.

In Puerto Rico there is a saying: "La luz de alante es la que alumbra," which means "The light in front is the one that guides." A lot of times this is used to encourage people to take advantage of the options they have. Roberto was that light for many people, and he knew it. Although he was frustrated by how little people recognized his talent, he knew how much good he could do while playing baseball. This made him want to succeed more, to prove himself and show Black, Latinx, poor, and struggling kids that they could do anything if they worked hard; that they could overcome obstacles, win, and be something no matter where they come from.

Roberto always enjoyed helping people, even when he was a kid—remember when he saved a man from a burning car at just twelve years old? He carried this spirit with him as an adult, too. Baseball became a way for him to amplify his humanitarian spirit, and he used it to give back to others every way he could.

During the off-season, he wore his Pirates uniform during baseball clinics he held for local children to help them develop their skills and confidence. He said, "I get kids together and talk about the importance of sports, the importance of being a good citizen, the importance of respecting their mother and father . . . Then we go to the ball field and I show them some techniques of playing

baseball." He stopped for any fan who asked for his time and would not leave until he had signed cards and spoken with each and every one. During his travel for games with the Pirates, he went through his fan mail to select letters from children in cities he would be visiting and dropped by his young fans in hospitals.

When he became more well known, especially among Puerto Ricans and other Latinx people, he received sponsorships throughout Latin America, and he donated all of those funds to charities. Eastern Airlines hired him as a sports adviser to promote the company and, in exchange, they sponsored baseball clinics for underprivileged Puerto Rican and other children. Sometimes while traveling, he would start the day off with a bag full of change and give it out to the people in need he met throughout the day.

Roberto also looked for others who made a difference. He felt a connection with Dr. Martin Luther King Jr. in particular, one of the Black leaders of the civil rights movement in the 1960s. Roberto marched in civil rights protests and eventually hosted Dr. King at his farm in Puerto Rico, near the rain forest El Yunque. When Dr. King was killed in 1968, Roberto was responsible for moving back the start of the baseball season to honor Dr. King and his legacy.

THE UNITED STATES AND THE CIVIL RIGHTS MOVEMENT

The civil rights movement began as a mass protest movement against racial segregation and discrimination in the United States that came to a boiling point in the mid-1960s and continues to this day. This movement is the result of centuries of racial oppression against enslaved African and Afro-descendant people, long after slavery was legally abolished.

Although formerly enslaved people were guaranteed basic civil rights after the Civil War through the Fourteenth and Fifteenth Amendments to the US Constitution, Black people are often still denied these rights. This is why Black-led movements like Black Lives Matter continue the work of the civil rights movement and earlier efforts to fight the economic, political, and cultural oppression that Black people face to this day.

Everything Roberto did was in service of others, both within and outside of baseball. This included serving his country, the United States. While other players relaxed and took vacations in the off-season, Roberto enlisted in the United States Marine Corps Reserve. Puerto Ricans have a rich history of military service, and Roberto's brother Matino, the "best baseball player in the family," had also served with the United States Army.

As with everything else in his life, Roberto did things his way. He wanted to serve his country, even though he could not sit at a table to eat a burger with his white teammates in many states, and even though he and other American citizens living in Puerto Rico could not vote for president because Puerto Rico did not and still does not have that right.

During basic training, Roberto broke records for the most chin-ups and for the fastest time maneuvering through the obstacle course. Roberto was one of only six others, out of 130 platoon members, to be promoted to private first class. He spent the next six years with the marines—while also playing major-league baseball.

CHAPTER FIVE

THREE THOUSAND— NO MORE AND NO LESS

"He gave the term 'complete' a new meaning. He made the word 'superstar' seem inadequate. He had about him the touch of royalty."

—BOWIE KUHN, former MLB commissioner

There's another popular saying in Puerto Rico: "No puedes tapar el cielo con la mano," which translates to "You can't cover the sky with your hand." This means you cannot deny what is obvious by pretending it doesn't exist.

As much as baseball's reporters, coaches, and leaders wanted to deny it, Roberto was a uniquely talented player, and eventually they would have no choice but to recognize him the way his fans did. After his historic play in the 1960 World Series and his eighth-place finish for most valuable player, Roberto was more motivated than ever.

Over the course of eighteen seasons with the Pittsburgh Pirates, Roberto would. play in fifteen All-Star Games; win twelve—*in a row*—Gold Glove Awards (honoring each league's best defenders at each fielding position) for his work in right field; win four National League batting titles

(awarded to the player with the highest batting average, or success rate of hitting a ball while at bat); win the National League's Most Valuable Player Award in 1966; become the highest-paid player in Pittsburgh Pirate history in 1967; and play 2,433 games for the Pirates, breaking the record for most games played by a Pirate.

Roberto had matured as a player and played baseball year-round most years. During spring training in Florida, Roberto continued to stay with the young players in "Pirate City," even though he could now afford to stay in nicer accommodations. He did this mainly for the young Latinx players who were on the mainland as he once had been, away from their families, surrounded by mainly English speakers, in the South. He had once been in their shoes and did not forget what it felt like.

So he stayed with them in Pirate City to teach them how to communicate with their teammates and how to order their meals. He made sure they felt welcomed and not alone. Roberto once said, "I believe that every human being is equal, but one has to fight hard all the time to maintain that equality." If he could make someone else's fight for equality easier, he made sure to do it.

Roberto also grew and thrived outside of baseball. In 1963, when he was twenty-nine years old, Roberto met a shy young woman who also dreamed of improving the world she lived in. Almost as soon as he met her, Roberto declared that he would marry her. She was the love of his life and his greatest confidant. A little less than a year later, Vera Cristina Zabala and Roberto Clemente married. Thousands of Puerto Ricans and others on the island clamored outside the San Fernando Church, where three hundred or so guests witnessed the union on November 1, 1964. The guest list highlighted all the sides of Roberto—in addition to his beloved family, Roberto's best friend, Phil Dorsey (a postal clerk in Pittsburgh), and the Governor of Puerto Rico, Luis Muñoz Marín, attended.

Together, Roberto and Vera would have three sons: Roberto Jr., Luis Roberto, and Roberto Enrique.

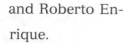

Roberto trusted and relied on Vera completely, telling his friends that he trusted her opinion above anyone's and that she had a better sense

FEMINISM IN THE 1960S

The women's rights movement of the 1960s fought for equal rights and opportunities for women along with greater personal freedom. Unlike the fight for women's right to vote in the early twentieth century, this movement touched on every aspect of life: work, family, politics, sexuality, even sports. Despite the gains women had made in the work force during World War II, cultural attitudes about women's role in society and the home continued to reinforce inequality in pay and job opportunities. Activists fought for and eventually won access for women to every corner of the job market. Record numbers of women began running for public office, and in 1972 Congress passed Title IX, the law that requires federally funded schools to provide athletic programs for women and girls.

Unfortunately, the women's rights movement had its own internal divisions. White members of the effort often excluded women of color and trans women because of the racism and queer phobia that was and is ever present. While decades later they still haven't achieved true equality, white women benefited the most from the gains of the movement, especially those in middle- and upper-class households, while women of color continued to be subjected to discrimination.

than him about whether he could trust people. One of his friends thought it was silly to trust a woman so much—there were laws in 1964 that did not even allow women to open bank accounts by themselves. He told his friend, "The way you think about women is what happened with the major leagues and Black players; they were afraid that if you let Black players in, they'd take over. That's the way you are with women."

Roberto's Pittsburgh Pirate teammates in the early years thought of him as quiet and shy. Many of those team-mates did not speak Spanish and did not try to show Roberto they were deserving of his friendship— after all, they were the same team-mates who will-ingly enjoyed the benefits of being white in the South while knowing that Ro-berto and others would be excluded. What some of his early teammates did not know is that Roberto could also be passionate and animated. One of Roberto's closest friends once said, "Conversing with Clemente is something that never ends."

Roberto played the harmonica, especially while driving. He made pottery and studied woodworking, collecting driftwood on local beaches. He wrote poetry, including these first two lines of a poem he wrote one Father's Day after he and Vera had started their family:

¿Quién soy yo? Soy un pequeño punto en el ojo de la luna llena.
Sólo necesito un rayo de sol para entibiar mi rostro . . .

Who am I? I'm a small point in the eye of the full moon.
I just need a ray of sunshine to warm my face . . .

Roberto's teammates and coaches in the later years seemed to know and understand Roberto—the player, poet, musician, artist, woodworker, husband, father, and friend—better than others had.

In July 1970, Melchor braved his first flight—at eighty-seven years old—and went to Pittsburgh. The Pittsburgh Pirates were honoring his son with Roberto Clemente Night, a bilingual (half in English and half in Spanish) and bicultural event for which Melchor, Luisa, and many others gathered in Pittsburgh to celebrate Roberto.

The event honored Roberto "as the complete ball-player, a legitimate super-star, and a polished performer with the glove and with the bat." On the field where the ceremony took place, the team had placed a life-size wax figure of Roberto. Other players might have accepted gifts, along with the praise. But not Roberto. He asked that any gifts intended for him instead be donated as money to the local children's hospital.

When it came time for Roberto to acknowledge the ceremony, he took a moment to dedicate the honor "to all the Puerto Rican mothers." He continued: "I've sacrificed these sixteen years . . . due to the effort it takes for someone to try to do the maximum in sports and especially the work it takes for us, the Puerto Ricans, especially for the Latinos, to triumph in the big leagues. I have achieved this triumph for us the Latinos."

Just as Roberto changed, the world around him was also changing. When Roberto first came to the mainland United States, he was one of only two Black players, and one of only two Spanish speaking players. He dreamed of one day playing as one of nine nonwhite teammates on the field. By the 1971 season, there were thirteen Latino and Black players on the team. And on September 1, 1971, during a game with the Philadelphia Phillies, the Pirates became the first team in Major League Baseball history to have a starting lineup of all Black and Latino players, with Roberto as their leader. This would not be Roberto's final historic feat.

The Pittsburgh Pirates had once again earned their spot in the World Series. The Baltimore Orioles were defending champions, having won the World Series the year before. Everyone thought the Pirates were going to lose. Yet again, most people were not paying attention to Roberto.

Roberto was mad, but this time it was a good kind of mad. It drove him to pursue what so few people thought was possible—another Pirates World Series win. But the night before the 1971 World Series between the Pirates and the Orioles, Roberto was sick. He had gone out to eat at a restaurant and ordered clams that turned out to be spoiled. By the time he returned to his hotel, the team doctor declared him so weak and dehydrated that he needed fluid and nutrition delivered directly to his veins through a noodle. Still weak the next morning, nothing would stop Roberto from playing. This wasn't a healthy choice, but Roberto felt the pressure of the entire team on his shoulders, regardless of whether that was fair.

The first two games of the series went as expected by most: The Orioles won. Even though the Pirates were losing, Roberto continued to give his all. During one play, he one-handedly caught a ball hit deep in right field and threw it back to third base, where the ball arrived just as the player formerly on second base did. One player said, "[Roberto] was in another zip code in right field . . . He turned around and this ball got to me pretty . . . quick. Usually a ball would take three or four hops from that spot in the outfield. He threw an absolute cannon." Another player said it was the best throw he had ever seen. Roberto's Pirate teammates knew this was just Roberto being Roberto.

The Pirates won the third, fourth, and fifth games in the series. Roberto had so many hits, one player observed, "How to pitch [to] Clemente? There was no way . . . [H]e'd hit anything. We couldn't get him out." The Pirates lost the sixth game and, like in 1960, the Pirates would play a tie-breaking seventh game of the series. By this point, journalists were taking notice of the oldest player in the series, at thirty-seven years old: Roberto.

Right before the last game of the series, people observed Roberto speaking with each of the team's players, one by one. He told each of them not to worry, they were going to win. The Pirates looked to their leader, and they believed him. When Roberto hit a home run to score the first run, the Pirates *really* believed him. One of his teammates hit another run, and the Pirates won the final game 2–1—they had won the World Series *again*!

This time, people noticed Roberto. He had a .414 batting average during the series, played beautiful games night after night, and was the first Spanish-speaking player selected as the World Series' most valuable player. When journalists approached him to hear his thoughts on his historic win, he said: "I would like to say something for my mother and father in Spanish. En el día mas grande de mi vida, para los nenes la bendición mía, y que mis padres me den mi bendición en Puerto Rico." This means: "On the biggest day of my life, I give my children my blessing and ask my parents to give me their blessing in Puerto Rico." This was the first time anyone had spoken Spanish live on national television in the United States, and Roberto did it as he seemed to do everything during that World Series—with confidence and ease.

At the start of the Pirates' 1972 season following their World Series win, Roberto knew he was close to something only ten baseball players before him had accomplished and that few players even dream of. Roberto was close to his three thousandth regular-season hit (hits during postseason games like the World Series do not count). Of those ten players before him, only three had reached that milestone since 1943. Roberto started the 1972 season with about 118 hits to go. He would be the first Latino player to reach this milestone and the third Black player, and he was determined to reach it. He said, "To get three thousand hits means you've got to play a lot . . . to me it means more. I know how I am and what I've been through. I don't want to get three thousand hits to pound my chest and holler, 'Hey, I got it!' What it means is I didn't fail with the ability I had. I've seen lots of players come and leave. Some failed because they didn't have the ability. And some failed because they didn't have the desire."

The fans were determined for him to reach it, too. On September 28, Roberto achieved his 2,999th hit, and his team pulled him from play so he could hit three thousand with his Pirates hometown fans in Pittsburgh. On Septem-

ber 29, Roberto and the Pirates played in Pittsburgh. The crowd gave Roberto a standing ovation when it was his turn to hit. This was it! Three thousand! He swung at a fast ball and barely touched it, but the scoreboard marked it as a hit. The crowd went wild. Then the game's official scorer stood up and declared, "Error." The hit didn't count. The next day, September 30, 1972, the Pirates played in Pittsburgh against the New York Mets. When Roberto's turn to bat came, he hit his hardest, as he always did. THWACK!

The ball took off toward left field, and Roberto had made history. Later, when the inning was over, Roberto turned toward the fans, took off his helmet, and raised it into the air.

After his historic season, many people asked if he would retire. Roberto said, in response, that so long as he could work, he would. "I don't care if I'm a janitor. I don't care if I drive a cab. As long as I have a decent job, I will work." He continued, "I make a lot of money, but at the same time I live the life of the common fellow . . . I am a shy fellow and you see me with the same people all the time . . . I just worry that I be healthy and live long enough to educate my sons and make them respect people. And to me this is my biggest worry: to live for my kids to be people that people look at them and respect them and they respect other people." Roberto dreamed of opening a "ciudad deportiva" in his future retirement, a sports city for Puerto Rican children where they could learn sports and gain self-confidence.

During the winter season, Roberto and Vera spent three weeks in Nicaragua getting to know and connecting with the people and the culture. He had visited previously in 1964 with the San Juan Senadores, when Nicaragua hosted the inter-American baseball winter series. Lots of exciting things happened during his visits, like when an overexcited fan threw a garrobo lizard from the right field bleachers, giving Roberto quite the scare. While in Nicaragua, Roberto had promised his sons he would adopt an animal for them—and he came back with a monkey!

In 1972 Roberto was managing Puerto Rico's baseball team during the world amateur baseball championship,

not playing. Roberto believed that "any time you have an opportunity to make a difference in this world and you don't, then you are wasting your time on this earth."

Each day during this trip, when others might focus on sightseeing or shopping, Roberto left his hotel with a bag full of coins to search out people who most needed it. He spoke and made connections with some of the neediest people in Nicaragua, and he'd come back to the hotel each night with an empty bag. During this trip he also visited local children's hospitals, as he often did, and helped raise money for a little boy who badly needed a wheelchair. After a memorable trip, Vera and Roberto returned home to Puerto Rico to celebrate Christmas with his sons and family.

Fourteen days after his return, he learned of a violent earthquake affecting Managua, Nicaragua's capital, where he had just spent several weeks. When Roberto and Vera heard about the earthquake, they thought of the many friends they had left behind just days before and knew they had to help. The earthquake left hundreds of thousands of people homeless. Major hospitals and hotels, the presidential palace, and the main fire station had all collapsed or been destroyed. Roberto was devastated. And he immediately got to work.

Roberto was selected to be the honorary chairman of an earthquake relief group. He knew that just because of who he was, the people would listen to what he had to say. He took advantage of his fame to bring attention to the horrible situation in Nicaragua and gather donations for the hundreds of thousands of people who now had no food, shelter, clothing, or medicine.

As with everything else in his life, Roberto dedicated himself entirely to this mission. He and Vera worked tirelessly, from early in the morning until late in the evening. They knocked on doors, staffed volunteer stations for gathering and sorting supplies, and organized a massive effort to activate people on the island to help Nicaraguans in need. In a matter of days, the group had collected twenty-six tons of food, clothing, and medicine, which they sent to Nicaragua by boat and airplane. Roberto thought these badly needed resources would go to the people who needed them most—but then he learned that the local military leader was taking the deliveries for his own purposes. None of the people Roberto wanted to help actually received what he had spent hours upon hours gathering for them. Roberto knew what he had to do, as he often did. And it was not the easy choice, as it often was not.

EARTHQUAKE IN MANAGUA

Around 12:30 a.m. on December 23, 1972, a 6.2-magnitude earthquake struck the heart of Nicaragua's capital, Managua. Of the city's three hundred thousand residents, two-thirds were displaced from their homes and thousands lost their lives. While headlines around the world proclaimed things like CAPITAL BATTERED, neighboring and nearby countries began to gather resources to help the Central American nation recover.

Not only did the earthquake destroy downtown Managua, but damaged pipes limited the water supply, and fires quickly spread throughout the city from downed power lines, electrical malfunctions, and gas leaks.

Almost immediately Nicaragua's military government declared martial law, suspending the ordinary law of the land and replacing it with strict military law involving curfews and other ordinances meant to control chaos. The criticism was quick. Within days, reports began circulating that former president Anastasio Somoza Debayle and his cronies in the government were embezzling the aid sent to Nicaragua by concerned countries, including the United States. To ensure the supplies made it to their intended destinations, Roberto Clemente decided to personally fly to Nicaragua, where he had visited just a few weeks before.

Roberto felt that if he personally accompanied the next flight of donations, there was no way the military leader would try to steal them. Not from Roberto Clemente. And not with the media's eyes on them. On New Year's Eve, December 31, 1972, Roberto prepared to board a DC-7 plane he had engaged on short notice to fly to Nicaragua filled with another batch of donations. Other Major League Baseball players on the island for the winter league offered to join him, but Roberto turned them down. He wanted them to be able to enjoy the New Year's celebrations.

Roberto still had a fear of flying, much like his parents, despite all the travel required by baseball, but he set all that aside to focus on helping people who needed it. He knew he had an opportunity to make a difference, and he did not intend to waste his time on this earth. Roberto knew the plane he had commissioned was brimming with important, life-supporting resources. They had packed it with hundreds of packages of rice, evaporated milk, beans, vegetable oil, meats, cornmeal, sugar, toothpaste, toothbrushes, and medical supplies.

But Roberto did not know that they loaded the plane without tying down this heavy cargo and without accounting for the plane's center of gravity. Roberto also was not aware that the pilot was on the verge of losing his pilot's license, that he had not slept the night before their flight, that he had a history of transport violations, or that he'd engaged an inexperienced copilot and flight engineer.

The plane's crew also lied on the plane's paperwork, saying it was about seven hundred pounds under the plane's limit, but in reality, they had loaded the plane with at least four thousand pounds more than its maximum allowed weight. One observer noted that the plane's landing tires looked squashed from the weight. Roberto had no idea the plane had been involved in an accident a short time before his flight. He trusted the pilot's word that Roberto would be taken care of, and that was enough.

As the plane rolled down the runway for takeoff, observers noted that it seemed to be struggling to gain speed. One person heard loud noises coming from the left wing. The plane finally got off land, but almost immediately after taking off from Puerto Rico's international airport, the plane fell into the ocean.

Roberto was thought to have died in the crash near Playa Piñones in Loíza, the home municipality of his mother. When Vera arrived on the beach near the suspected crash site, she realized that it was one of Roberto's favorite places to collect wood.

Vera, their boys, the entire island of Puerto Rico, the Pittsburgh Pirates, the baseball community, and the countless people Roberto had helped during his short time on earth mourned his loss deeply. The Puerto Rican governor, Luis A. Ferré, declared a three-day period of mourning, a time to honor his memory and allow people to grieve. Shortly after, a newly inaugurated governor, Rafael Hernández Colón, said about Roberto, "Our youth have lost an idol and an example; our people have lost one of their glories." President Richard Nixon, an avid base-ball fan who had called Roberto "unbelievable" after his second World Series performance, kept close tabs on the search and rescue operations. Some people on the island, including major-league players, spent days searching the shorelines near the crash site, trying to hold on to hope that the majestic, magical Roberto Clemente would some-how find his way back home.

CHAPTER SIX

PITTSBURGH'S BORICUA PIRATE

"We really had no idea that history was being made."

—AL "SCOOP" OLIVER, MLB outfielder, first baseman, and seven-time All-Star

On April 17, 1955, at just twenty years old, Roberto Clemente played his first major league game with the Pittsburgh Pirates. They were facing the Brooklyn Dodgers.

Roberto played right field and batted third. He was known to be smart but let his brilliance shine on the field. He could gauge exactly how he needed to hit the ball to accomplish his team's goals at any point in the game. That day, Roberto hit the first of his three thousand hits.

Each of those three thousand hits required Roberto to

determine how the ball had been pitched, where the out-fielders were positioned and who they were, how fast he and his teammates could get around the bases, how the weather might affect his hit, and more.

On July 25, 1956, after little more than a year with the Pirates, Roberto hit the first and only documented inside-the-park grand slam walk-off in baseball history. If it had been up to the team's manager at the time, it never would have happened! After Roberto hit the ball, he sprinted from base to base. Pirates manager and third-base coach Bobby Bragan signaled at Roberto to stop running, but Roberto knew he could make it to home plate. According to one reporter, Roberto dashed toward home, "slid, missed the plate, then reached back to rest his hand on the rubber," giving the Pirates their tie-breaking ninth run. The crowd went "goofy with excitement," even though the Pirates manager was not happy Roberto had ignored his signal.

After four years with the Pirates, Roberto still struggled to receive proper recognition for his achievements in the league, but in May 1960, he received the National League's Player of the Month Award for the first time. He would win twice more during his eighteen-year career, in May 1967 and July 1969.

MAJOR LEAGUE BASEBALL'S TWO LEAGUES

Most professional sports have leagues throughout the world. Formed in 1903, the oldest of these sports leagues is Major League Baseball (MLB), which consists of thirty teams as of 2022. These teams are divided between the National League (formed in 1876) and the American League (formed in 1901). During the World Series, the winning team from each league competes with each other in a series of seven games.

In October 1960 the Pittsburgh Pirates went into the World Series as the underdogs—most people in baseball thought they would lose to the American League's New York Yankees. Instead, the Pirates fought hard across seven games and won!

Roberto, ever strategic, knew how to make the game work for him. Yankees pitcher Whitey Ford faced Roberto twice during the series. After the series, Whitey realized that Roberto purposefully hit poorly against an outside ball, in order to fool Whitey into pitching another outside ball the next time Roberto was at bat. "I did . . . and he unloaded."

Roberto hit a .310 batting average during the series and had three runs batted in—known as RBIs, which means a player's hit is credited for a run. Roberto had hits in every single game and gave the nation a taste of the energy, passion, and skill with which he played. He was also the first Latino starting-position player to win a World Series.

Roberto felt he should have been voted the Most Valuable Player after his incredible performance, including a vital hit in the final game's eighth inning that helped put the Pirates in the lead. Instead, this honor went to one of his teammates. Roberto was disappointed and frustrated that his talent was not getting the recognition he felt it deserved.

After his historic World Series performance that year, Roberto was selected for the first of fifteen MLB All-Star Games—from 1960 through 1967 and 1969 through 1971, with two games per season from 1960 to 1962. During the All-Star Games, the greatest talents from each of the National and American Leagues play against one another in an exhibition game usually held in July. In 1960 Roberto had the fourth-highest batting average in the league with .314 and had hit sixteen home runs and ninety-four RBIs.

Roberto's selection was proof that his talent was being recognized beyond Pittsburgh, but he still felt the sting of the 1960 World Series MVP selection.

The following year, Roberto won his first National League Silver Bat batting title for achieving the highest batting average in his league. Recipients receive a heavy silver-plated bat engraved with their signature and the batting average that earned them the award. The leagues calculate batting averages by dividing the number of a player's hits by the number of times they were at bat. Roberto won the National League's batting title four times: in 1961 he won the Silver Bat with a batting average of .351, in 1964 with .339, in 1965 with .329, and in 1967 with .357.

But it was not just his batting average that impressed— it was the way in which he hit as well. After one 1966 home run, the opposing team's pitcher said, "I threw him a fastball, low and inside, and he hit it into the upper deck in right field . . . He amazes me." He also ran strategically. One reporter observed how Roberto "showed the fans how to run bases" and, even though the opposing team had the ball to tag him out, Roberto "waited until [the player] made his move, then jumped over him and touched home plate with his hand."

Roberto's right field acumen thrilled fans and, in 1961,

earned him the first of his twelve consecutive Gold Glove Awards. He is tied with one other player for the most Gold Glove Awards earned by an outfielder. Managers and coaches from each team vote for the players who have excelled in their particular position, though they cannot vote for players on their own team. Roberto consistently took an all-or-nothing approach to the outfield that other teams, players, and fans grew to recognize. His "acrobatic" style meant Roberto could leap, slide, or run backward. His ability to catch ball after ball was proof of his talent, work ethic, and spirit. In one game, Roberto reportedly "threw himself at the ball and grabbed it inches above the ground as he rolled on the turf." He would do whatever it took to catch the ball, even if it meant risking injury to himself. Of course, these injuries meant Roberto was frequently in pain and could not play as often as he (or his fans) would have liked.

Time and again, Roberto overcame challenges. He still suffered from pain after his 1954 car accident and other injuries, but Roberto *still* managed to achieve the most home runs (29) and RBIs (119) of his career. Finally, on November 16, 1966, Roberto was the first Latino player to be selected as the most valuable player in the National League. The MVP award was chosen by twenty baseball writers using a points system, not total votes. Roberto won the award with

218 points—ten points ahead of the second-place player. Roberto said of his selection, "It's the highest honor a player can hope for, but I was expecting it."

Off the field, Roberto showed that he was an advocate for himself and others, often using his voice and resources to help those around him. In 1967 he negotiated his salary with the Pirates to become the highest paid player in Pirate history. The Pirates reportedly agreed to pay him $100,000, which is the equivalent of approximately $860,790 in 2022. Although that is certainly a lot of money, it is much less than many professional baseball players earn today. In many ways, Roberto paved the way for others to ask for proper compensation for themselves, not just in baseball.

The Pirates' new ballpark, Three Rivers Stadium, opened on July 16, 1970. Eight days later, the stadium hosted the Pirates' Roberto Clemente Night, honoring Roberto in front of forty-three thousand fans. The ceremony was conducted half in English and half in Spanish. More than two hundred of Roberto's family, friends, and fans from Puerto Rico flew up for the ceremony, including Roberto's eighty-seven-year-old father, who worked with a psychiatrist to overcome his fear of flying and board the plane to Pittsburgh. Some of the youngest travelers included children from Puerto Rico who won contests to attend the event. The ceremony was also broadcast in Puerto Rico and featured everything from Spanish songs about Roberto to a life-size wax figure. He told a reporter that day, "In a way, I was born twice. I was born in 1934 and again in 1955, when I came to Pittsburgh. I am thankful to say that I lived two lives."

Of course, we know what Roberto did. He turned the event—which was supposed to be all about him—into a fundraiser for Pittsburgh's Children's Hospital. People presented Roberto with a variety of gifts, supplies, a television, luggage, jewelry, a set of winter car tires, and even a new car! There were so many gifts that they brought a truck onto the newly finished Three Rivers turf to take

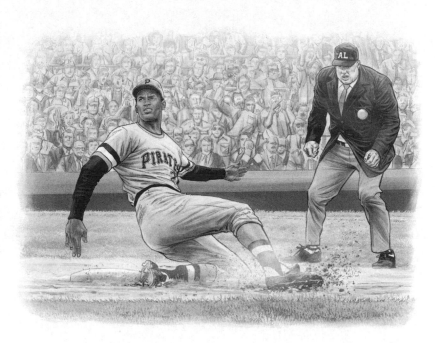

everything away. The event raised $5,500 (the equivalent of almost $41,000 in 2022), which Roberto wanted to go to poor families who could not afford to pay for their children's medical expenses.

After the ceremony, the Pirates played against the Houston Astros. Roberto hit twice and made a memorable play when he slid into a gravel track while running to catch a ball, cutting open his knee. When he walked off the field for medical attention, the crowd gave him his fifth standing ovation that evening.

THE PIRATES' FIRST
ALL-BLACK LINEUP

On September 1, 1971, eight Black baseball players took the field at Three Rivers Stadium.

Starting Pitcher: Dock Ellis
Catcher: Manny Sanguillen
First Base: Al "Scoop" Oliver
Second Base: Rennie Stennett
Third Base: Dave Cash
Shortstop: Jackie Hernandez
Center Field: Gene Clines
Left Field: Willie Stargell
Right Field: Roberto Clemente

Clemente, Hernandez, Sanguillen, and Stennett were Latino.

It took *twenty-four years* from Jackie Robinson's entering the major leagues to the first all-Black lineup. Unsurprisingly, this lineup included Roberto. On September 1, 1971, Roberto and his Black Pirates teammates, including three other Black Latino players, faced the Philadelphia Phillies. One player noted that "to us, it was no big deal, because we had so many minorities on our team," in stark contrast to Roberto's first few years in the league. Another player thanked "Clemente's influence," which allowed the Pirates that year to "show that you could have stars that are Black and whose clubhouse culture was rooted in accepting everyone on equal footing."

Much like in 1960, the Pirates were not expected to win when going up against the Baltimore Orioles in the 1971 World Series. But the Pirates did it—again! Roberto hit a staggering .414 batting average during the series, had four RBIs and two incredible home runs, and made a crucial hit in the last game that helped secure the Pirates' win. He again hit in every single game of the series. This time, his performance did not go unrecognized. Roberto was the first Latino selected for the series' Most Valuable Player honor.

A few months later, on January 29, 1972, Roberto received his eleventh Gold Glove Award. Unfortunately, that would be the last official league honor Roberto received during his lifetime. The MLB awarded Roberto his twelfth and final Gold Glove after his death, with Vera accepting on his behalf.

On September 30, 1972, Roberto became only the

eleventh player in major league history—and the first Latino—to reach three thousand hits. When his hit was counted, the crowd went wild, and the umpire had to delay the game while fans cheered and clapped for several minutes. Roberto did not know what to do with himself, saying, "I feel bashful when I get a big ovation . . . I am really shy. I never was a big shot and I never will be a big shot." While speaking with reporters after his historic game, Roberto dedicated his three thousandth hit "to the Pittsburgh fans and to the people in Puerto Rico, and to one man in particular," his first coach, whose encouragement led him to this milestone. Roberto's three thousandth hit ended up being his final hit of the season and of his entire career, since the MLB does not count postseason hits toward career statistics.

After eighteen years, Roberto played his last game as a Pittsburgh Pirate during the National League's championship series, on October 11, 1972. He had played 2,433 games as a Pirate, tied with one other player for the most games in Pirate history. At the end of his career, Roberto had a .317 batting average, 240 home runs, 1,416 runs scored, and 1,305 RBIs. He left Pittsburgh for Puerto Rico, where he would coach the San Juan Senadores in the Puerto Rican league during his off-season. Although

Roberto sometimes hinted at an impending retirement, he intended to play with the Pirates in the next season.

Roberto often spent the off-season hosting baseball clinics for kids in Puerto Rico, as he one day hoped to do upon retiring. In November the Puerto Rico Telephone Company sponsored five clinics for children. When Roberto found out that there were more children than spots, he asked his sponsor to host an additional clinic in Agua-dilla, a town on the northwest side of Puerto Rico. On November 27, during a batting demonstration, Roberto hit the last known home run of his life in front of the three hundred children in attendance. He gifted his bat to one of the children and the ball to another.

CHAPTER SEVEN

ROBERTO'S LEGACY

"That night on which Roberto Clemente left us physically, his immortality began."

—ELLIOTT CASTRO TIRADO, Puerto Rican
writer and sports commentator

None of Roberto's accomplishments happened overnight. He worked hard, day by day, night by night, to shape who he was on the field and off. Roberto's legacy, what he's remembered for, is something Vera, their sons, and many others have worked tirelessly to preserve and grow.

Immediately after his death, Vera and others mobilized to honor Roberto by helping the Nicaraguans he had been trying to help when he lost his life. Two days after the accident, President Nixon released a statement saying: "[Roberto] sacrificed his life on a mission of mercy. The best memorial we can build to his memory is to contribute generously for the relief of those he was trying to help: the earthquake victims in Nicaragua." President Nixon also worked with the Pittsburgh Pirates to set up a memorial fund for Roberto and personally donated a $1,000 check to get it started.

During this time, the Baseball Writers' Association of America (BWAA) was also working on something nearly unheard of. The BWAA is responsible for selecting and electing players to the Baseball Hall of Fame. Among other rules, only players who have been inactive in baseball for five years or more are eligible for selection.

On January 3, 1973, just three days after Roberto's death, the BWAA announced that it would amend its rules to allow a special election for Roberto. They had started the process to induct Roberto into the Hall of Fame, waiving the rule that a player is only eligible after being inactive for five years. This rule had been set aside only once before, to honor famed New York Yankees first baseman Lou Gehrig, who was very ill and had retired from baseball in 1939 after being diagnosed with ALS (amyotrophic lateral sclerosis), and died two years later from the terrible disease shortly after his special election.

Joe Heiling, the president of the BWAA, noted that Roberto "would have been elected and inducted in his first year as an eligible. So why wait?" Even before Roberto was officially eligible for selection, writers were returning their ballots for that year's election with his name written on them. The BWAA requires at least 75 percent of the vote to elect players to the Hall of Fame. Roberto was elected with 93 percent of the more than 400 BWAA writers voting in his favor. So, on March 20, 1973, less than three months after the crash, Roberto became the first Latino player to be elected to the Baseball Hall of Fame.

Roberto Clemente was inducted into the Baseball Hall of Fame on August 6, 1973.

Vera accepted on Roberto's behalf, saying, "This is a momentous last triumph, and if he were here, he would dedicate it to our people of Puerto Rico, our people in Pittsburgh, and to all his fans through- out the United

States." In speaking about Roberto, Bowie Kent Kuhn, the MLB commissioner, said:

> So very great was he as a player, so very great was he as a leader, so very great was he as a humanitar ian in the cause of his fellow men, so very great was he as an inspiration to the young and to all of us in baseball and throughout the world of sports, and so very great was his devotion to young people every- where and particularly to the young people of his native island of Puerto Rico. Having said all those words, they are very inadequate to describe the real greatness of Roberto[.]

Roberto's childhood hero, Monte Irvin, was inducted on the same day.

On April 6, 1973, the Pittsburgh Pirates retired Roberto's uniform number, number 21, during opening day ceremonies at Three Rivers Stadium, where Roberto Clemente night had been celebrated less than three years before. Roberto had played all eighteen seasons of his MLB career with the team.

From 1973 until 2000, the Baseball Hall of Fame misiden- tified Roberto as Roberto Walker Clemente, instead of Roberto Clemente Walker, since they were not used to Latinx naming conventions. During a visit, Vera saw their mistake, and in 2000 the Hall of Fame cast a new bronze plaque for Roberto to correct it. The Hall of Fame has only done so a few times, including for Roberto's predecessor, Jackie Robinson. Jackie's original plaque did not mention Jackie's historic role in ending segregation in baseball—the very integration that allowed Roberto to join the major leagues.

On May 14, 1973, a little over four months since the crash, President Nixon awarded the first Presidential Citizens Medal to honor "distinguished Americans for their service." The president selected Roberto as the very first recipient of that medal, which was given to Vera in Roberto's place. He said, "All who saw Roberto Clemente in action, whether on the diamond or on the front lines of charitable endeavor[s], are richer for the experience. He stands with that handful of men whose brilliance has transformed the game of baseball into a showcase of skill and spirit, giving universal delight and inspiration. More than that, his selfless dedication to helping those with two strikes against them in life blessed thousands and set an example for millions. As long as athletes and humanitarians are honored, Roberto Clemente's memory will live; as long as Citizens Medals are presented, each will mean a little more because this first one went to him."

That same day, Congress enacted a new law that authorized the creation of one gold commemorative medal in honor of Roberto, and 200,000 duplicates whose sales would help fund the Roberto Clemente Memorial Fund. This would not be the last time a US president honored Roberto. In 2003, when Roberto would have been sixty-nine years old, President George W. Bush awarded Roberto the Presidential Medal of Freedom, saying: "He was a young man with a quick bat, a rifle arm, and a gentle heart."

Over and over again, Vera and her sons honored Roberto's legacy. Roberto had long dreamed of opening a ciudad deportiva, a sports center for Puerto Rico's at-risk children. When he died, Vera endeavored to make this dream a reality. In 1974, she and other passionate Puerto Ricans seeking to conserve his legacy and pass on the lessons he taught in life opened up the Ciudad Deportiva Roberto Clemente in Carolina, a 304-acre sports city that includes baseball and soccer fields; tennis, volleyball, and basketball courts; a pool; and more. At one point, the center had more than 100,000 annual visitors. In 2017, Hurricane Maria devastated the island and, along with it, the already-aging ciudad deportiva.

In May 2012, the Puerto Rico winter league where Roberto got his start changed its name to the Liga de

Béisbol Profesional Roberto Clemente (the Roberto Clemente Professional Baseball League). The name was changed to honor what Roberto meant for baseball in Puerto Rico and Latin America, as well as to symbolize a partnership with Roberto's family to help further Roberto's dreams for the Ciudad Deportiva.

Beginning in 1973, the year after Roberto's death, the Major League Baseball's Commissioner's Award became the Roberto Clemente Award. Each year, the league honors a player who exhibits Roberto's values, including "his commitment to community" and the importance of helping others. It's an annual reminder of who Roberto was and serves as an inspiration to players even now. Every September, each team nominates their most deserving player. A panel, that includes Roberto's now-adult children, selects the winner out of the thirty nominees. The award is announced during the World Series.

In 2018, Yadier Molina, a Puerto Rican baseball catcher for the St. Louis Cardinals, received the Roberto Clemente Award following his relief efforts in Puerto Rico for victims of Hurricane Maria, which had ravaged the archipelago in September 2017. He said, "When I was growing up he was like a legend for us, like a hero, and he was

everywhere . . . He was one of my heroes back in the day—still one of my heroes—and just to have this award means a lot to me and to my family." He also said, "For all us Latinos who have played Major League Baseball and have had to deal with so many obstacles, difficulties, and challenges, Clemente is the source of inspiration we need to move forward and pursue our dreams, and be an example to others on and off the field[.]"

September 15 is the first day of National Hispanic Heritage Month, and as of 2021, it is officially celebrated as

Roberto Clemente Day. The Pittsburgh Pirates, Puerto Rican players, players who have won the Roberto Clemente Award, managers, coaches, and others honor Roberto by wearing his number 21. Among other events, the Pittsburgh Pirates honored Roberto's legacy by engaging in community service projects. In 2022, in honor of the

fiftieth anniversary of Roberto's death, the MLB allowed for all prior award winners to wear a number 21 patch on their caps and sticker on their helmets, beginning on opening day of the 2022 season and for the rest of their careers.

Even years after his death, Roberto's talent and achievements in baseball and off the field continue to be recognized. All throughout Puerto Rico, the mainland United

States, and the world, people have named their schools, parks, coliseums, scholarships, awards, and more in honor of Roberto. In Liberia, a one-dollar coin honors Roberto and his 1973 Hall of Fame induction.

One school in Orlando, Florida, originally opened in 1965 as a school only for white students. The community named it after Stonewall Jackson, a general with the Confederacy in the United States' civil war. In 2020, the school board voted unanimously to rename it the Roberto Clemente Middle School after students suggested new potential names and the community voted on their top choices. Even then, forty-eight years after his passing, Roberto's memory continued to build upon the civil rights movement and empower young people to dream beyond what they know.

Roberto used his incredible baseball skills and accomplishments to help reach people. Over time, his many efforts grew into something bigger than himself. Children learned to love baseball and other sports because of the passion he had for his own. He inspired some to accomplish what no one has done before. He moved others to help people and make a difference, to not "waste their time on this earth." How will *you* make the most of your time here?

DID YOU KNOW?

✧ Roberto's full name was Roberto Enrique Clemente Walker. Early in his career, many would use "Walker," his mother's last name, as Roberto's.

✧ Roberto Clemente ranks among the best professional baseball players of all time. He received the Most Valuable Player Award, twelve Gold Glove Awards, four National League batting titles, twelve All-Star Game selections, two World Series Championships, and reached the 3,000-hit milestone. Only ten major league players had recorded 3,000 hits before Roberto.

robertoclemente.si.edu/english/virtual_legacy.htm

✧ Clemente's batting average was .317.

baseballhall.org/hall-of-famers/clemente-roberto

✧ Clemente became the first Hispanic to speak Spanish on a live network television broadcast when he thanked his parents after the final game of the 1972 World Series.

aarp.org/entertainment/celebrities/info-2021/roberto
-clemente.html

✧ After Roberto Clemente's death, the MLB's Commissioner Award changed its name to the Roberto Clemente Award. It is given out to the player who "best exemplifies the game of baseball, sportsmanship, community involvement, and the individual's contribution to his team."

defense.gov/News/Feature-Stories/story/Article/2717641
/sports-heroes-who-served-corps-infantryman-was-one-of
-baseballs-greatest/

✧ Clemente wore number 21, which was retired by the Pittsburgh Pirates in 1973.

defense.gov/News/Feature-Stories/story/Article/2717641
/sports-heroes-who-served-corps-infantryman-was-one-of
-baseballs-greatest/

✧ A cenotaph (a monument erected in honor of a person whose remains could not be recovered) by José Buscaglia was installed in Carolina, Puerto Rico, to honor Roberto Clemente's life.

robertoclemente.si.edu/english/virtual_legacy.htm

✧ After Jackie Robinson, Clemente became the second baseball player to be depicted on a US commemorative postage stamp, first in 1984, then again in 2000 in the Legends of Baseball Classic Collection.

vc.bridgew.edu/hoba/8/

✧ Roberto Clemente enlisted in the US Marine Corps Reserve after the 1958 season and spent six months on active duty at Parris Island, South Carolina, and Camp LeJeune, North Carolina. He served until 1964 and was inducted into the Marine Corps Sports Hall of Fame in 2003.

defense.gov/News/Feature-Stories/story/Article/2717641
/sports-heroes-who-served-corps-infantryman-was-one-of
-baseballs-greatest/

✧ Clemente was inducted to the Major League Baseball Hall of Fame in 1973, just a year after his death, when voters in a special election waived the mandatory five-year waiting period between when a player retires and when they can be added to the Hall of Fame.

baseballhall.org/hall-of-famers/clemente-roberto

✧ Roberto Clemente's batting helmet has been in the Smithsonian collections since 1981. His jersey and bat are featured in the Smithsonian's Latino Center digitization project, which allows people to view them via the museum's narrated augmented reality (AR) experience.

americanhistory.si.edu/press/releases/%E2%80%
9C%C2%A1pleibol%E2%80%9D-slides-smithsonian-fall-2020

americanhistory.si.edu/latinos-and-baseball

A NOTE FROM SARA E. ECHENIQUE

It is one of the greatest privileges of my life to be able to raise my children with an immense sense of pride in their Puerto Rican heritage and a sense of connection to my home. Hand in hand with that pride is the sense of responsibility in continuing the legacy of our greats (of which there are many), like Roberto Clemente. This year (2022) marks the fiftieth anniversary of Roberto's three-thousandth hit and of his plane crash. Even though Roberto passed away years before I was born, his is a story that I and other Puerto Ricans are lucky to inherit. When I was in fourth grade or so, Vera Clemente visited my school and spoke about Roberto. What I most remember is the passion with which she spoke and clearly lived her life. It's only fitting that this book comes out as my oldest child enters the fourth grade, as I hope it provides the opportunity for another generation of children to learn about, know, and be inspired by Roberto and all he achieved in his short time on earth.

In addition to thanking my parents, siblings, husband,

and children for their steadfast support (and everything else that would need a full tome to scratch the surface), I want to extend my boundless gratitude to the incredible individuals who made this possible, including Claudia Romo Edelman and Hispanic Star for this opportunity, the Roaring Brook Press team for their guidance, and my agent, Marietta Zacker, for her support and wisdom.

A NOTE FROM HISPANIC STAR

When Hispanic Star decided to join Macmillan and Roaring Brook Press in creating this chapter book biography series, our intention was to share stories of incredible Hispanic leaders with young readers, inspiring them through the acts of those Stars.

For centuries, the Hispanic community has made significant contributions to different spaces of our collective culture and everyday life—whether it's sports, entertainment, art, politics, or business—and we wanted to showcase some of the role models that made this possible. We especially wanted to inspire Hispanic children to rise up and take the mantle of Hispanic unity and pride.

With Hispanic Star, we also wanted to shine a light on the common language that unifies a large portion of the Latinx community. *Hispanic* means "Spanish speaking" and frequently refers to people whose origins are from a country where Spanish is the primary spoken language. The term *Latinx,* in all its deviations, is broader and more inclusive, referring to people of all gender identities from all countries in Latin America and their descendants, many of whom were born in the United States.

This groundbreaking book series can be found both in English and Spanish as a tribute to the Hispanic community in our country.

We encourage all our readers to get to know these heroes and the positive impact they continue to have, inviting future generations to learn more about the different journeys of our unique and charming Hispanic Stars!